My World of Science

WATER

Angela Royston

Heinemann
LIBRARY

www.heinemann.co.uk/library
Visit our website to find out more information about **Heinemann Library** books.

To order:
☎ Phone 44 (0) 1865 888066
▤ Send a fax to 44 (0) 1865 314091
🖥 Visit the Heinemann Bookshop at www.heinemann.co.uk/library to browse our
catalogue and order online.

First published in Great Britain by Heinemann Library, Halley Court, Jordan Hill, Oxford,
OX2 8EJ, a division of Reed Educational & Professional Publishing Ltd. Heinemann is a
registered trademark of Reed Educational & Professional Publishing Ltd.

OXFORD   MELBOURNE   AUCKLAND   JOHANNESBURG   BLANTYRE
GABORONE   IBADAN   PORTSMOUTH NH (USA)   CHICAGO

Designed by bigtop, Bicester, UK
Originated by Ambassador Litho Ltd.
Printed and bound in Hong Kong/China

05 04 03 02 01
10 9 8 7 6 5 4 3 2 1

ISBN 0 431 13703 X

British Library Cataloguing in Publication Data
Royston, Angela
Water. – (My world of science)
1. Water – Juvenile literature
I. Title
553.7

Acknowledgements
The Publishers would like to thank the following for permission to reproduce photographs:
Collections: John Callan p11; Corbis: pp5, 6, 7, 14, 15, 17, 24, 27; Eye Ubiquitous: p18; Robert Harding:
p29; Robert Royston: p8; Still Pictures: Toby Adamson p25; Stone: pp20, 28; Trevor Clifford: pp4, 9, 10,
12, 13, 16, 19, 21, 22, 23, 26.
Cover photograph reproduced with permission of Stone: Ray Massey.

Every effort has been made to contact copyright holders of any material reproduced in this book.
Any omissions will be rectified in subsequent printings if notice is given to the Publisher.

Contents

What is water? 4

Where water comes from 6

Water for life 8

Using water 10

Flowing water 12

Ice and water 14

Heating water 16

Steam 18

Drying 20

Floating and sinking 22

Light for its size 24

Water pushes back 26

Moving through water 28

Glossary 30

Answers 31

Index 32

Any words appearing in the text in bold, **like this**, are explained in the Glossary.

What is water?

Water is usually a liquid. A liquid does not have a shape of its own. It takes the shape of its **container**. Which of these containers holds the least water?

Water is a clear, runny liquid. But water can also be a solid piece of ice and steam in the air. Ice is very cold, and steam is very hot.

Where water comes from

When it rains, water **flows** off the land into streams and rivers. Streams and rivers flow across the land into the sea.

water evaporates

rain

Some of the water in the sea and in rivers **evaporates**. This means it changes into gas. This gas floats into the air and forms new rain clouds.

Water for life

People, plants and animals all need water to stay alive. Some farmers spray their plants with water to make them grow better.

All food has water in it. Fruit and vegetables have lots of water in them. Squeeze an orange to see how much juice you can get. Most of it is water.

Using water

We use water at home for washing clothes, dishes, ourselves and other things. Soap makes things easier to wash.

Firefighters use water to put out fires.
They pump the water on to the flames
through long hosepipes.

Flowing water

Water always tries to **flow** downhill.
The **steeper** the slope, the faster
water flows. What will happen if this
girl tips the bottle more?

Water cannot flow uphill on its own.
When you drink through a straw,
you have to suck the water up into
your mouth.

Ice and water

When water becomes very cold, it changes into ice. Ice is a solid and so keeps its shape. This statue has been cut from a huge block of ice.

Thermometers measure **temperature** in degrees. Water always freezes and melts at 0 degrees **Celsius**. These icicles are melting.

Heating water

When water is heated, it slowly turns into gas. When it reaches 100 degrees **Celsius**, it begins to boil. Be careful – boiling water **scalds**.

Bubbles of gas form in the water. The bubbles rise to the top of the water and burst. The gas drifts up into the air.

Steam

You cannot see the gas in the air, but you can see steam. Steam is made when water gas turns back into tiny water **droplets**.

Water droplets form at other times
too. If you breathe on to a mirror, it
will become misty. The mist is made of
tiny water droplets.

Drying

Wet hair can be dried with a hairdrier. The water in your hair slowly changes into gas. The gas drifts into the air and your hair dries.

These children are measuring the size of a puddle as it dries up. They measure it every 20 minutes. It gets smaller and smaller as it dries.

Floating and sinking

Some things are very light. They float when you put them into water. You can test different things to see which ones will float.

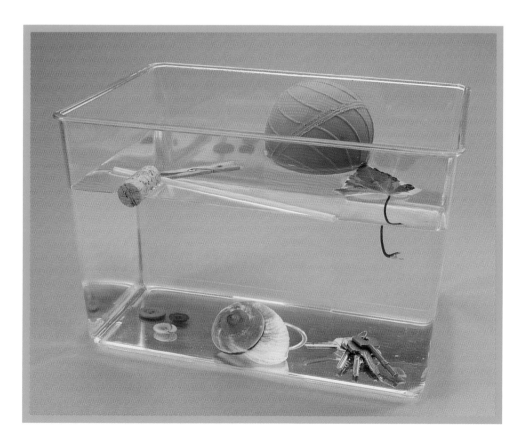

The heavy things will sink to the bottom of the bowl. Which of these things were too heavy to float?

Light for its size

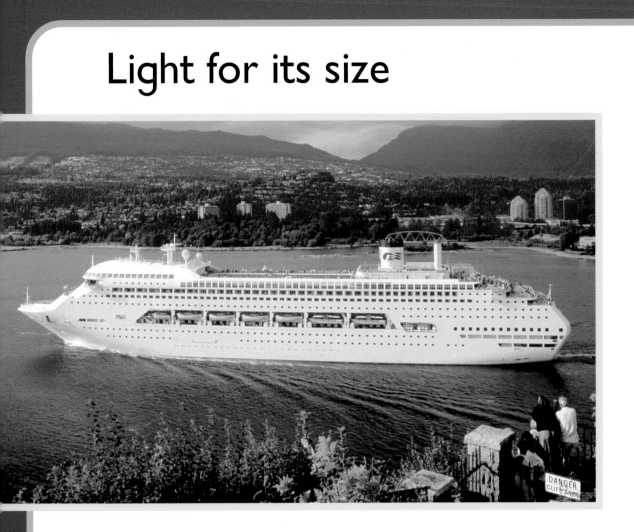

Something floats if it is light for its size. This ship is big and heavy and yet it floats. That is because it is filled mainly with air, and air is very light.

These heavy logs are floating on the river. Wood floats because there is lots of air trapped inside it.

Water pushes back

When you put something into water, it pushes some of the water away. The water then pushes back! This balloon is difficult to push under the water.

When you lie on water, the water pushes up and makes you float. This is just like when the water pushed back against the balloon.

Moving through water

To move through water, you pull the water backwards and the water pushes you forwards. When you swim, your hands and arms pull the water back.

Boats also move forwards by pulling the water backwards. These people pull the paddles back to push the canoes forward. Moving through water is fun!

Glossary

Celsius scale for measuring temperature

container something that you can put things in – for example, a box or jar

droplet very small drop

evaporate when liquid water changes into gas

flow to move smoothly

scald to injure like a burn but with very hot water or steam

steep when a slope rises or falls very sharply

temperature how hot or cold something is

thermometer something that measures temperature

Answers

Page 4 – What is water?
The tallest, thin glass holds the least water.

Page 12 – Flowing water
The water will flow faster if the girl tips the bottle more.

Page 23 – Floating and sinking
The shell, keys and buttons were too heavy to float.

Index

evaporating 7
farmers 8
firefighters 11
floating 22–25, 27
gas 7, 16–17, 18, 20
ice 5, 14
puddles 21
rain 6, 7
sea 6, 7
ships 24
steam 5, 18
streams and rivers 6
swimming 28
thermometer 15
washing 10
water droplets 18–19